IMPRESSIONS *of the*

YORKSHIRE
MOORS & DALES

Produced by AA Publishing

© Automobile Association Developments Limited 2007

Published by AA Publishing (a trading name of Automobile Association
Developments Limited, whose registered office is Fanum House, Basing View,
Basingstoke, Hampshire RG21 4EA; registered number 1878835)

ISBN-10: 0-7495-5212-3
ISBN-13: 978-0-7495-5212-1

A03033B

A CIP catalogue record for this book is available from the British Library.

Colour reproduction by KDP, Kingsclere
Printed and bound in Thailand by Sirivatana Interprint Public Co Ltd

Opposite: a typical dales landscape of barns and drystone walls.

IMPRESSIONS *of the*

YORKSHIRE
MOORS & DALES

Picture Acknowledgements

The Automobile Association would like to thank the following photographers, companies
and picture libraries for their assistance in the preparation of this book.

Abbreviations for the picture credits are as follows: (AA) AA World Travel Library

F/C AA/T Mackie; B/C AA/T Mackie; B/C inset AA/T Mackie; 3 AA/T Mackie; 5 AA/D Tarn; 7 AA/M Kipling; 8
AA/M Kipling; 9 AA; 10 AA/M Kipling; 11 AA/D Tarn; 12 AA/M Kipling; 13 AA/T Mackie; 14 AA/J Morrison; 15
AA/S & O Mathews; 16 AA/M Kipling; 17 AA/T Mackie; 18 AA/M Kipling; 19 AA/M Kipling; 20 AA/J Morrison;
21 AA/M Kipling; 22 AA/T Mackie; 23 AA/M Kipling; 24 AA/T Mackie; 25 AA/M Kipling; 26 AA/M Kipling; 27
AA/M Kipling; 28 AA/T Mackie; 29 AA/M Kipling; 30 AA/T Mackie; 31 AA/M Kipling; 32 AA/T Mackie; 33 AA; 34
AA/L Whitwam; 35 AA/T Mackie; 36 AA/T Mackie; 37 AA/M Kipling; 38 AA/T Mackie; 39 AA/M Kipling; 40
AA/T Mackie; 41 AA/T Mackie; 42 AA/P Baker; 43 AA/T Mackie; 44 AA/T Mackie; 45 AA/J Mottershaw; 46 AA/D
Tarn; 47 AA/T Mackie; 48 AA/M Kipling; 49 AA/T Mackie; 50 AA/T Mackie; 51 AA/M Kipling; 52 AA/T Mackie;
53 AA/D Tarn; 54 AA/T Mackie; 55 AA/J Morrison; 56 AA/M Kipling; 57 AA/M Kipling; 58 AA/T Mackie; 59
AA/M Kipling ; 60 AA/M Kipling; 61 AA/T Mackie; 62 AA/T Mackie; 63 AA/J Morrison; 64 AA/D Tarn; 65 AA/M
Kipling; 66 AA/T Mackie; 67 AA/A Baker; 68 AA/T Mackie; 69 AA/M Kipling; 70 AA/T Mackie; 71 AA/M Kipling;
72 AA/M Kipling; 73 AA/M Kipling; 74 AA/L Whitwam; 75 AA/T Mackie; 76 AA/T Mackie; 77 AA/M Kipling; 78
AA/T Mackie; 79 AA/J Morrison; 80 AA/J Mottershaw; 81 AA/M Kipling; 82 AA/T Mackie; 83 AA/M Kipling; 84
AA; 85 AA/T Mackie; 86 AA/D Tarn; 87 AA/M Kipling; 88 AA/M Kipling; 89 AA/S & O Mathews; 90 AA/T
Mackie; 91 AA/M Kipling; 92 AA/T Mackie; 93 AA/T Mackie; 94 AA/M Kipling; 95 AA/T Mackie.

Every effort has been made to trace the copyright holders, and we apologise in advance for any unintentional omissions
or errors. We would be happy to apply the corrections in any following edition of this publication.

Opposite: the distinctive landscape of Upper Wharfedale in the Yorkshire Dales.
Many of the fields were enclosed by drystone walls at the beginning of the 19th century,
but their origins may go as far back as the iron age.

INTRODUCTION

There is so much variety in Yorkshire's landscape, that it would be impossible to try to capture it all in one slim volume of pictures. So here we have selected a series of images that reflect the dales and moors, which for many, have become a byword for the whole county. But even with that choice, we're still in a vast region, from the green fields of Dentdale, to the pantiled rooftops of Staithes, spilling off the North York Moors into the North Sea, and from the airy crags of Otley's Chevin and Ilkley's iconic Cow and Calf to the peaceful vale of Pickering. Within this space lie two National Parks, the Yorkshire Dales, and the North York Moors, and three Areas of Outstanding Natural Beauty (AONBs) – the North Pennines, the Howardian Hills and Nidderdale. Most of this region lies in North Yorkshire, but it can get confusing. The more easterly of the two National Parks is to the north of York, a position which gives rise to its name – the 'North York' Moors. There are dozens of lovely dales in the North York Moors, but the Yorkshire Dales (also mostly in North Yorkshire) are in another place altogether – the western side of our Yorkshire region.

All this naming of names is meant to help you navigate from dale to dale, and this need for navigation is a crucial part of the moorland experience. High on the heathery expanses above Eskdale or Farndale, Bransdale or Bilsdale, you'll find ancient crosses, waymarkers from generations of travellers who crossed this landscape without modern vehicles. Some of those travellers were traders to the fishing villages that clung to the treacherous North Sea coast, others would have traded wool from the extensive monastic estates. You can't escape the influence of the great monasteries here. Not only did the monks of Fountains, Rievaulx, Jervaulx,

Byland, Bolton and the rest leave their ruins as architectural waymarks to the skill of medieval craftsmen, but their development of sheep farming in these sometimes inhospitable uplands left an industry which survives even today. Perhaps that is something to ponder as the sheep attempt to eat your sandwiches on Sutton Bank or Pen-y-Ghent. Fittingly, the logo of the Yorkshire Dales National Park is the head of a Swaledale tup (a male sheep), and the North York Moors takes its identity from an ancient cross, known as Young Ralph, which stands in graceful solitude above the bogs and heather near Rosedale Head.

It is sometimes forgotten that the North York Moors National Park includes over 30 miles of dramatic coastal scenery. From the artists' village of Staithes to the busy bays of Scarborough, there is coastal scenery to rival that found anywhere in Britain.

The Cleveland Way National Trail links this clifftop world of sweeping bays and tumbling villages to the spacious heights of the Cleveland escarpment in the west. From here the views stretch far across the Plain of York to a skyline which inspired another of England's great walking routes. The Pennine Way links the watershed tops that run through the heart of the Yorkshire Dales, passing Malham Cove and Pen-y-Ghent among other well-loved places.

There are so many moors and dales that to visit them all would take a lifetime. And then you would want to start all over again.

A solitary standing stone adds mystery to the heather moors above Fryupdale.

The Upper Falls at Aysgarth, Wensleydale.
Opposite: Rievaulx Abbey, which is now run by English Heritage,
was one of the wealthiest monasteries in medieval England.

Rowing practice in Whitby's Inner Harbour. The annual Whitby Regatta has attracted rowers from all over the North for more than 100 years.

Field barns near Grassington. Known locally as laithes they are typical of Upper Wharfedale's landscape.

New Road, Robin Hood's Bay connects the upper end of this little fishing village to the seafront.

*Evening light on a hawthorn tree in the limestone uplands around
Ingleborough in the Yorkshire Dales.*

St Margaret's Church commands an elevated position above Hawes, Wensleydale.
Opposite: upland hay meadows near Muker, Swaledale – rare survivors of more intensive farming.

An ancient waymarker on the moors above Hutton-le-Hole.

A wayside waterfall in Dentdale in the north west of the Yorkshire Dales National Park.

Seen from Stoop Brow, Ravenscar, the blue sweep of Robin Hood's Bay ends in the cliffs of Ness Point.

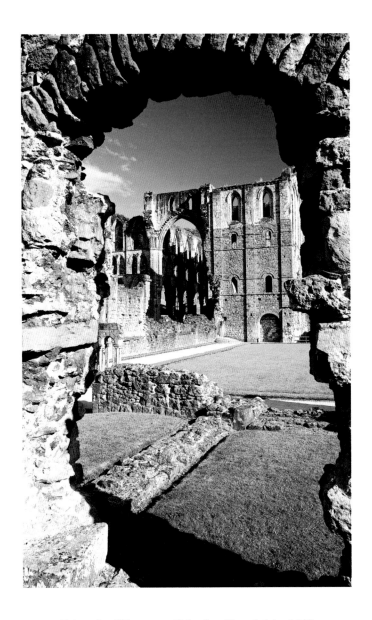

Rievaulx Abbey near Helmsley. Founded in 1133,
it was the first Cistercian house in the north of England.

The paved meadow path to the parish church in Hawes, Wensleydale.

Robin Hood's Bay is laced with narrow alleyways between the fisherman's cottages.

On the Cleveland Way National Trail, near Robin Hood's Bay.
Opposite: Ribblehead Viaduct on the Settle–Carlisle railway. Its 24 arches across
the bleak terrain of Batty Moss took four years to complete.

Brimham Rocks, Nidderdale. Rain, ice and wind have conspired to make this remarkable landscape of gritstone shapes and pillars, some more than 20ft (6m) high.

Looking into the Hole of Horcum, a vast natural amphitheatre at the heart of the North York Moors.

The White Horse of Kilburn, on the scarp of the Hambleton Hills, was completed by volunteers in 1857.
Opposite: sunset silhouettes Rievaulx Abbey.

Lower Wharfedale and the Plain of York, stretch away beyond Otley from the crags of its famous Chevin.

A gateway in the 17th-century walled garden at Nunnington Hall near York.

The North York Moors Association Millennium Stone, above Rosedale.
Opposite: the village of Muker, surrounded by meadows, near the remote head of Swaledale.

A rose-covered cottage in lovely West Burton. The village boasts one of the largest village greens in Yorkshire.

The limestone cliffs of Malham Cove. At the end of the last ice age, there would have been a vast waterfall here – the Niagara of the Yorkshire Dales.

Pillars in the ruined choir indicate the former majesty of Rievaulx Abbey.
Opposite: morning mist hangs in the fields near Hawes, Wensleydale.

At the heart of Skipton Castle stands a venerable yew tree, planted by Lady Anne Clifford in 1659.

Roseberry Topping rises from the mists at the northern tip of the North York Moors.

The Yorkshire Dales landscape is indebted to the hardy sheep.

The 19th century brought a colony of artists to tiny Staithes on the North Sea coast.

Lovely Dentdale, in the north west corner of the Yorkshire Dales National Park.

The bridge over the River Swale at Muker, Upper Swaledale.

Richmond's impressive 11th-century castle is one of the oldest stone-built fortifications of its type in the country.
Opposite: the familiar profile of Pen-y-Ghent from the boardwalk route of the Pennine Way.

Though in ruins, Knaresborough Castle retains some delightful medieval details.

Low tide in Whitby harbour. Captain Cook set sail to Australia from here in 1768.

Baled straw ready for collection in a field near Pateley Bridge, Nidderdale.
Opposite: the spectacular vaulted cloister roof at Fountains Abbey.

Cowbar Cottage and a tiny fishing boat, Staithes.
The village's fishing fleet was once one of the biggest on the east coast.

The bracken covered slopes of Embsay Crag rise above the reservoir on the southern edge of the Yorkshire Dales National Park.

Long, thin, wispy clouds, high over fields near Askrigg in Wensleydale.

Borough Beck winds through the centre of Helmsley,
on the edge of the North York Moors.

Drystone walls are a familiar feature of the Dales landscape.
Opposite: the Strid, near Bolton Abbey, Wharfedale. This treacherous rapid in the River Wharfe
is barely 6ft (2m) wide and has claimed many lives.

Ragwort flourishing on fallow land in Swaledale.

The distinctive pantiled roofs of Robin Hood's Bay, seen from the top of the cliffs behind the village.

Roseberry Topping's hard sandstone cap has protected the underlying shale and clay, producing its distinctive shape.

Beck Isle Cottage and Thornton Beck, a much photographed corner of Thornton-le-Dale, near Pickering.

A meadow of buttercups near Fangdale Beck in Bilsdale.
Opposite: the ten arches of Dent Head Viaduct on the Settle–Carlisle line.

The Board Inn, and Lealholm's bridge over the River Esk, Eskdale, North York Moors.

'Grikes', the fertile gaps in between the 'clints' of a limestone pavement.

A haze of spray from Walden Beck at the falls in West Burton, Wensleydale.

Rievaulx Abbey, on the edge of the North York Moors, was dissolved in 1538 and passed to the Earl of Rutland.

Pebbles and a limpet shell on the beach at Runswick Bay.
Opposite: descending into Swaledale from the Buttertubs Pass, between Hawes and Thwaite.

Looking under the bridge at Gunnerside, the River Swale is at a low summertime level.

Grassington's cobbled streets retain an air of historic authenticity.

Late 17th-century Newby Hall, near Ripon, is still a family home.

Egton's stone bridge over the River Esk was rebuilt in 1992,
in the style of the original, which was washed away in the 1930s.

The Abbey Steps, 199 in all, link Whitby's east cliff and abbey with the town.
Opposite: in mysterious How Stean Gorge, Nidderdale, you can believe in fairies and trolls.

Looking into Danby Dale in the North York Moors, from the crags on Castleton Rigg.

A signpost in the market place in Helmsley.

Rosedale's calcinations kilns are a reminder of the region's ironstone mining past.

Field barns like this one in the Yorkshire Dales have found new uses as bunkhouses, offices and homes.

The ruined priory at Bolton Abbey in Wharfedale.
Founded in 1151, building work was still underway on Dissolution in 1539.
Opposite: flat-topped Easterside Hill rises above Bilsdale, North York Moors.

Aysgarth Falls in Wensleydale. These picturesque cascades have appeared in several films, including Robin Hood: Prince of Thieves *from 1991.*

Byland Abbey's monks moved from West Cumbria in 1177 and earned much of their wealth from farming sheep in the Hambleton Hills.

Rain sweeps across Ryedale near Helmsley.

Pantiled buildings huddle round the inner harbour at Whitby.

Sheep scatter down a lane, near Greenhow Hill, on the moors between Nidderdale and Wharfedale.

Kettle Ness from the Cleveland Way National Trail: this much quarried headland forms the southern end of Runswick Bay.

A cow stands guard over her gate in Muker, Upper Swaledale.

Opposite: Semer Water in Raydale, above Wensleydale, is the largest natural body of water in Yorkshire.

Ilkley's Cow and Calf Rocks. Legend claims that these massive gritstone crags were split apart by the giant Rombald.

Helmsley's town hall and market cross, Ryedale.
There has been a market on this site since the 15th century.

Looking across to Ravenscar from Robin Hood's Bay.

Opposite: both farming and mining have shaped the landscape of Upper Swaledale.

Looking down on the River Nidd and the dramatic rail bridge from Knaresborough's 12th-century castle.

The ruins of St Hilda's Abbey, Whitby were an inspiration
for Bram Stoker's Dracula story.

Knaresborough Castle suffered greatly for being a Royalist stronghold in the Civil War.

Near West Burton, where Bishopdale and Waldendale meet Wensleydale.

Old Ralph's Cross is one of several waymarks on the high moors
between Castleton and Rosedale in the North York Moors.
Opposite: sunrise in the Yorkshire Dales above Ribblehead.

INDEX